CHRIS MARR

Become an Authoritative Coach

Stop people pleasing, challenge your clients, and be indispensable

First published by The Authoritative Coach 2023

First edition

ISBN: 978-1-7395080-0-5

Cover art by Col Gray at pixelsink.com

This book was professionally typeset on Reedsy.
Find out more at reedsy.com

Contents

PRAISE FOR BECOME AN AUTHORITATIVE COACH

Chris has been the most impactful mentor I have had in my professional career. This work is a fantastic high level summary of the things I've learned that changed the way I work. I highly recommend reading this so you can change the way you think about client work and how you can make a difference by becoming a coach under Chris's tutelage - ***Lara Black**, Certified They Ask, You Answer Coach, www.commonmind.com*

A truly solid guide to the coaching mindset was precisely what I was seeking when I became a coach. This is a really valuable guide from Chris. A vital foundation. - ***Nick Burrage**, Managing Director and Certified They Ask, You Answer Coach, www.theambitionsagency.com*

This great summary contains highly valuable insights that will change the way you work with clients forever. By following Chris's deep knowledge and wise advice, I have not only reduced stress and pressure at work, I have also become more respected and valued by my clients. Highly recommended. - ***Magnus Brynestam**, CEO and Certified They Ask, You Answer Coach, Sweden. www.grown.se*

Chris is a shining example of someone who embodies the philosophy of becoming an indispensable coach. His training has had a dramatic effect on my career and helped me navigate the changing landscape and relationship between agency marketers and their clients. I now truly believe that if you want to redefine your relationship with clients, and truly become an authoritative figure, then Chris is the person to speak to and learn from. - ***Tom Wardman***, *Certified They Ask, You Answer Coach, www.tomwardman.com*

Through coaching with Chris, you can expect to unleash an ability to listen, think, react and communicate more intentionally than you ever have. If used correctly, this method of coaching and communication can transform your career and leave others surrounding you wondering how you're doing it. I'll never go back and I promise, after you begin applying the principles in this booklet - you won't want to either. - ***Megan Miller***, *Revenue Enablement Manager, www.atsinc.com*

So much of becoming indispensable to our clients is our mindset. I love how Chris digs into those places where our mindset often goes astray and undermines our authority with our clients. He then firmly and graciously leads us where we need to go so we can be the best for your clients, your family, and yourself. It's not just about being a better coach, he helps us be better humans. - ***Steve Phipps***, *Marketing Coach & Fractional CMO, www.wayfindmarketing.com*

I had the pleasure of spending 6-months being coached by Chris. I had been struggling for years as a solo marketing consultant. I was so frustrated I almost walked away from marketing altogether. Chris showed me a better way, and now I have the confidence that I can be a better partner empowering clients, all while being able to maintain my sanity as a solo coach. Chris made a huge impact on me and my business, and I can attest that what he discusses in this book is exactly what he does in real life on coaching calls. And it works! - ***Darin "Doc" Berntson***, *CEO of Bernco Media & Certified They Ask, You Answer Coach, www.berncomedia.com*

Chris's approach to coaching has been transformative for me. Before working with him, my instinct was to take on the role of an advice-giver. However, Chris has guided me to embrace the true essence of coaching by teaching me the importance of asking questions first. His seasoned approach has expanded my perspective, and I have found myself growing not just as a coach but as a person. One of the most liberating and empowering lessons I've learned from Chris is the realisation that it's not about having all the answers. He has an innate ability to help you uncover the power of asking the right questions, which has changed the way I engage with my clients and has led to deeper, more meaningful interactions. - ***Danielle Navas-Brandt***, *Certified They Ask You Answer Coach, www.flynq.nl*

Of all the training I've sought out in my career, working with Chris tops the list as most impactful for how it's transforming the way I show up, communicate and lead personally and professionally. - ***Erin Fults***, *Brand Strategist & Marketing Coach, www.theacornteam.com*

All too often, business books feel derivative, filled with platitudes and obvious insights that make it easy to confuse one book with another. Think of Chris's work as the antidote to that. Every insight filling the following pages is hard-won and carefully considered. Chris draws on more than a decade of client experience to give you a leg up in your own coaching career. He is the consummate teacher: patient, creative, and thoughtful. Every lesson is clearly close to Chris's heart — and the product of deep reflection. And the value, in turn, is tremendous. - ***John Becker***, *M.S.Ed., Director of Content, www.impactplus.com*

In his new book, The Authoritative Coach, world-class communicator and coach Chris Marr, summarises incredibly valuable and hard-earned life lessons on how to be not only a better coach but also a better human. I am grateful and blessed to have Chris as my teacher and mentor and his teachings have not only shifted my entire mindset on coaching, but have had maybe the most profound impact on my professional development. Chris taught me to embrace and leverage that emotional tension created by committing to life-long learning and always wanting to become a better coach — something I mistook for weakness, self-doubt, and imposter syndrome in the past. Because only mediocre people are always at their best! - ***Hannah Eisenberg***, *CEO & Certified They Ask, You Answer Coach, www.3pcreativegroup.com*

Become an Authoritative Coach is THE book for anyone who deals directly with customers, clients, and even team members. Chris guides the reader through a process of transitioning from being a people-pleasing coach to one who commands authority, garners respect, and achieves outstanding results. As a former people-pleaser, working with Chris has elevated my coaching and leadership abilities to an entirely new level. I have no doubt that this book will have the same impact on anyone who reads it and diligently applies Chris' ideas. - ***Gavin Bell**, Director, Yatter, www.weareyatter.com/*

Imagine how far you could go as a 'coach' if your communication skills reach an entirely new level. A level where you guide everyone, from clients, employees, to your family, to discover and shape their own destiny, in the most impactful way possible. Chris is your perfect guide on this exciting journey. As he has done for me, he'll help you transform how you communicate, you'll attract more clients, better clients, and you'll realise your best work is ahead of you. This is your first step. Strap yourself in. - ***Mark Reynolds**, Digital Sales & Marketing Coach and Certified They Ask, You Answer Coach, www.ProfitReach.uk*

If there is one book on earth you should read on becoming an ACTUAL authoritative coach, leader, communicator, wife, husband, or just a person, then it is this book. The advice, insights, wisdom, and knowledge that comes from Chris Marr, are some of the best in the world. His simple but immensely powerful methods for building authority are exactly that simple and anyone can implement and feel like a BOSS. - ***Tasha Dal Bianco**, They Ask, You Answer Coach, www.RedPandas.com.au*

Every once in a while there arrives a book in a discipline that signals an evolution on how best to do things. They Ask, You Answer did this for marketing. Good to Great did this for business and leadership. Become an Authoritative Coach has done this for communication. In a way, Marr's title is misleading - it's not just for coaches. Coaching is communication and communication is at the heart of everything. It's there when you want an A-Player to work for you, it's there when you're pitching on that life changing deal. It's there when you're trying to understand your life partner when things aren't rosy. If you want to be seen as the expert you are, have authority in any human interaction no matter how big the alpha is and do so by being true to yourself - this is the book for you. Be kind yet resolute. Be blunt yet empathetic. Be intentional yet remain curious. Be an Authoritative Coach. - ***Moby Siddique***, *CEO, Red Pandas, www.redpandas.com.au*

Chris is a consummate professional and seasoned expert on the behaviours and mindset that distinguish a good coach from a great coach. If you want to become indispensable to your clients, then this is a guidebook not to be missed. - ***Linda Damico***, *Head of Content & Certified They Ask, You Answer Coach, Red Pandas, www.redpandas.com.au*

I have always considered myself more of a consultant than a coach. Even a previous coaching certification did not make me a coach as I considered myself the one who had to do the work for my clients. The work with Chris has changed this perspective, especially when it's the right time to be a coach and when it's the right time to be the consultant. What has changed for me is that I try to be a coach first to help my clients develop. So for anyone who is struggling with the same or similar issues this book is a great source of inspiration and guidance. - ***René Neubach***, *CEO, Content Glory, www.contentglory.com*

Business and marketing can be noisy and bewildering. The constant flood of strategies, tactics, apps and tech companies and individuals face can cause paralysis rather than growth. Chris has always been a calming influence in a hectic world and the calm and clarity he brings comes from the questions he asks. He helps companies find the answers they need for business success. In *Become an Authoritative Coach*, Chris unwraps his techniques for us and reading it becomes a journey of self discovery. Be prepared to answer the questions Chris poses and they'll help you find a path to personal and business success. - **Roger Edwards**, *Marketing Speaker and author of Cats, Mats and Marketing Plans, www.rogeredwards.co.uk*

Chris has pulled an incredible amount of experience and passion into this book. Through Chris's teaching I've both been at the hand of his coaching and began my own journey with his teachings. Being on the receiving end I can vouch that his teachings will grow you and your team in the most profound way. More authoritative coaches in the world please! - ***Nicola Hutchison***, *Sales and Marketing Director, Gillies and Mackay,* www.gilliesandmackay.com

I'm aware that my role is (or should be) more coach than consultant. It's a rare adviser who engages the client to look deeper into the causes of their need and within to find the actual solutions, which are always behavioural. *Become an Authoritative Coach* did what all the best such books do for me - they make me think, immediately, about how I can implement the suggestions into the work we do for our clients. That's why I need to go back through it now and make more notes! - ***Pete Matthew***, *Founder of MeaningfulMoney.tv and CEO of Jacksons.life*

ABOUT THE AUTHOR

CHRIS MARR, also known as The Authoritative Coach, is a renowned coach and mentor, based in the beautiful city of Dundee, Scotland. With over 1000s of hours of coaching experience with companies of all sizes, Chris has established himself as a true expert in his field.

As the Global Coaching Performance Director at IMPACT, Chris is responsible for leading, training, and coaching all They Ask, You Answer coaches across the world. He is the first certified They Ask, You Answer coach, demonstrating his commitment to staying at the forefront of his profession.

Aside from his extensive coaching background, Chris is also a Stoic Practitioner and Philosopher, fascinated by human behaviour and dedicated to studying anything and everything that can help him understand people better. Chris's passion for continuous learning and professional development is unwavering and evident in his ongoing pursuit of knowledge.

Chris's experience, expertise, and commitment to his profession make him one of the most sought-after coaches in the industry. With his knowledge and insights, he helps businesses and individuals achieve their full potential, and reach their personal and professional goals.

* * *

- Subscribe at www.theauthoritativecoach.co.uk[1]
- For speaking, podcast and coaching enquiries, email chris@theauthoritativecoach.co.uk[2]
- Connect with Chris on LinkedIn: @theauthoritativecoach[3]

DEDICATED TO...

Cara, My Queen.

"I wish you could see you like I see you"

DEFINITION

Authoritative *(adjective)*

Able to be trusted as being accurate or true; reliable. Commanding and self-confident; likely to be respected and obeyed.[4]

FOREWORD

Authority.

An interesting word indeed.

These days, it seems to get a bit of a bad rap.

Such is understandable though.

Not everyone uses authority the way it should be used.

For the sake of this conversation, though, we need to get quickly past this.

Why?

Because if you're going to become the best coach you can be, and if you're going to change lives the way you should, you MUST BECOME AN AUTHORITY with clients.

Not a peer.

Not a buddy.

Not a friend.

An AUTHORITY.

Respected over liked.

Understood over impressed.

Growth over comfort.

Reading this, you may feel such goals are obvious.

But for most coaches, they are not.

When I first met Chris Marr, such was the case.

He had all the right intentions.

His heart was clearly where it needed to be.

He truly wanted to change lives and elevate his clients to the best version of themselves.

But despite his best intentions, his impact on others was average.

Why?

Simply put, he wasn't an *authority* to his clients.

At least, not to the level he needed to be in order for them to do the things that would take them from good to great.

At times he chose to be liked.

In other instances, he sought to impress.

And on occasions, he chose comfort over real progress.

Keep in mind, none of this made Chris a bad coach.

In fact, he was pretty good.

But he wasn't GREAT.

He wasn't elite.

But that changed.

Just like it will change for you.

Without mincing words, let's be very honest with each other here:

You might find yourself wanting to resist some of what you read in this book.

You may feel certain teachings from Chris don't apply to you.

You may even think you do some of the things herein more effectively than Chris, himself, does them.

Please don't go down this road.

You are not different.

You are not the exception.

Nor am I.

Some people call me a world-class coach.

Yet there are elements of this book I consistently screw up.

To err is human, and unless each of us goes back to the well and keeps drinking, bad habits can form quickly in our behaviour.

This book is the well.

So, go back often.

Drink.

Receive what you read herein.

Not only will it change your life, but it will change the lives of your clients too.

Such is the power of this magical profession.

So here's to you becoming An Authoritative Coach.

Marcus Sheridan, Author of They Ask, You Answer[5]

July 2023

PROLOGUE

"You have to decide what your highest priorities are and have the courage pleasantly, smilingly, and non-apologetically – to say no to other things. And the way to do that is by having a bigger yes burning inside."

STEPHEN COVEY

I used to be a people-pleaser.

This was a behaviour that was hurting the success of my clients, the success of my team, and ultimately the success of my coaching business.

I was holding everyone back, including myself.

I needed to change the type of relationship I had with my clients.

They were in control. They were calling the shots.

The truth is, even though they never explicitly said it, my clients knew that they weren't getting what they needed. They didn't want a passive order taker, they wanted to be challenged.

I know most coaches struggle with this. For me, this is what it looked like:

- I said yes to requests I knew we couldn't do, or couldn't do well
- I said yes to projects that I knew would fail (or I made myself sick trying to make them work!)
- I let clients make mistakes and bad decisions that would hurt them in the short and long term
- I said yes to bad-fit clients and their bad behaviour

I felt like I couldn't say no to my clients.

We have to ask ourselves: What negative impact is this having on our people, our client results, the growth of our coaching business?

It's time to step up and challenge our clients. Make it clear that we're willing to walk away if we don't think true success is possible.

Now, years later, I've turned my past weakness into a strength that helps my clients:

- I ask the difficult questions others struggle with
- I call out the mistakes they are making
- I'm not afraid to say no

The result of this fundamental shift? Our clients step up and prove to us what they are capable of.

They become better, more successful clients.

We're doing better work, and I'm a better coach with a more successful coaching business.

I'm not saying it's easy, but it's for the best. For everyone involved.

This is what it means to Become an Authoritative Coach.

To leave our people-pleasing in the past, and become the coach our clients need us to be.

Let's get to work.

I

MINDSET

Becoming an Authoritative Coach begins with how you think about yourself, getting clear on the value you bring, and being self-confident and self-assured about your expertise. It's the mindset shift from friend to expert, amateur to professional, nice to kind, from being liked to being respected. For the shift to happen in your client relationships it has to happen for you first. Ultimately, your mindset limits your ability to coach your clients to be successful at their highest potential.

1

COACH VS CONSULTANT

"If you realize that all things change, there is nothing you will try to hold on to"

LAO TZU

Up until recently, I hadn't given this much thought.

Of course, I had a sense there was a difference between a consultant and a coach, but if you had asked me to spell it out for you, it would have been my first time articulating it.

Perhaps one reason we don't think there's much difference between the two is because they have quite a lot in common:

- Both are external to the client organisation
- Both are hired to solve problems
- Both come with their specific areas of expertise

Perhaps the most glaring reason we don't have a clear answer to this question is that we don't see how important it might be to take the time to think about it — to define each role and then compare them to each other.

But there are significant differences.

To illustrate, think about these distinctions:

- The **consultant** expresses opinions and advice
- The **coach** holds back on opinions and advice

- The **consultant** does all the thinking
- The **coach** helps the client do the thinking

- The **consultant** solves a specific problem
- The **coach** asks if we're solving the right problem

- The **consultant** has a limited scope
- The **coach** has an unlimited scope

- The **consultant** focuses on the business

- The **coach** focuses on the individual

- The **consultant** solves the business problem
- The **coach** enables people to solve the problem

- The **consultant** gives the solutions
- The **coach** helps the client discover the solutions

Now, everything is simple and straightforward when we talk in absolutes, and I'm sure you're thinking what I'm thinking — it's not quite as simple as that.

Arguably, a great consultant will also be able to perform some of the functions of a coach, as will a coach be able to consult.

And that's where we end up: We have to be both.

Yes, it's helpful for us to see the differences laid out like this. It gets us thinking about the two different approaches, but the real skill we have to develop is knowing when our client needs us to be a coach, and when they need us to be a consultant.

To know when to dig in with questions, and when to give advice and solutions.

To know when to say "What's holding us back from being

successful here?" and "Here's what you need to do..."

To dial in our self-awareness and read the room.

The not-so-obvious problem is that we end up consulting when we should be coaching, and vice versa.

It takes real discipline to be a coach. It's a lot easier to just tell the clients what to do.

After a coach friend of mine spent time thinking about the difference — especially in his own work. Here's what he said:

> *"I had a revelation which is the difference between consulting and coaching and I've probably spent 20 years consulting with passion...this has made me really step back and think...I made it a lot harder than it could've been. It's a huge difference for me and I'm really having to reassess just who I am and what I do. I've got to learn to step back and [let my clients] do the thinking and do the work...I'm probably still in way too active parent mode with my clients. And that's my challenge."*

It's not uncommon for professionals to have the realisation that they have been doing far too much consulting — taking on all the work, doing all the thinking for their clients, and ultimately making everything much harder for themselves.

Personally, the most dramatic shift in my professional life came when I embraced my identity as a coach, and more often than not, I'm leaving client sessions with nothing on my plate.

Personal reflection:

- How much consulting I am doing when I should be coaching?
- What will be my biggest challenge in shifting my mindset and approach to a more coach-like style?
- What kind of impact will it have on my work and my clients if I can be more of a coach for them?

Perhaps the most important question is: Who's doing most of the thinking? Me, or my clients?

2

WHO'S THE HERO?

"You cannot teach a man anything. You can only help him discover it within himself."

GALILEO GALILEI

If we want to be great coaches, we need to focus on developing two key traits.

1. We need to work on becoming genuinely curious about the person we're coaching
2. And we need to empower the person to act and grow

In other words, our role as a coach is to use our skills and knowledge to not look smart or serve ourselves but instead to serve the other person so they feel like they own it for themselves.

Too often we're coming into our coaching sessions:

- Knowing what the right answers are
- Knowing what the outcome should be
- Knowing what the conversation needs to look like
- Knowing what they need to say
- Knowing what they need to get

This is where many coaches get themselves tied up — they're holding on too tightly to the results and outcomes.

And so, what ends up happening is that the coach takes too much control. They are too invested in the outcome.

They end up making it about them.

They want to be the smartest person in the room.

One clear risk in all of this is that when your client starts to push back on you about even the tiniest thing, you feel defensive because you take it personally.

It's not about you

Part of being a great coach is knowing that it's not about you. That it's never about you.

Instead, to be a great coach, you need to:

- Let go of the need to be right
- Be comfortable letting the other person determine the outcome
- Allow the other to lead the conversation

- Listen deeply to what's really being communicated and allow that to guide your curiosity
- Create relationships that allow the other to get what they need

In short, you need to be comfortable not controlling every aspect, and not controlling other people — a difficult shift for many leaders and coaches.

What my experience tells me is that even those who believe they are great coaches are still essentially telling people what to do.

Often times it pays to ask yourself "Who's the hero in this story?" And of course, if we're world-class coaches, it should be the person we're helping that feels like the hero.

Personal Reflection

- How much time do I spend telling people what to do versus being genuinely curious?
- Am I holding on too tightly to what I think is the right thing for them to do?
- What would my coaching look like if the outcome was for them to own it and feel truly empowered?

3

THE PRIZE

"My soul no longer has that piquant activity conferred by desire...Oh, we shouldn't delude ourselves - pleasure isn't in the fulfilment, but in the pursuit."

PIERRE-AUGUSTIN CARON DE BEAUMARCHAIS

"The grass is always greener on the other side"

We've all said it a hundred times. It's human nature to look over the fence and desire exactly what you don't have. We all find pleasure in spending time imagining the other side of the fence.

At the same time we complain, gripe, and take for granted what we do have.

And this is happening every single day.

Think about the clients who object, slow down the sales process, pause, and ultimately never buy.

The clients who think they're done, but they've still got a lot of work to do.

The clients that end their contract early and hire your competition.

All of them, to some degree, lost their desire for you and the work. They started taking you for granted, and over time the value and respect they had for you diminished.

Hard to hear, I know.

And that's why you must lean into the human nature of 'the grass is greener' and make it so that you're something that your clients desire but can't easily obtain.

Your client looks over the fence, they see you there, but they have to work hard to get you.

This inspiring example from Mad Men will help paint a picture - go ahead and *watch it right now* (~2 mins)[6].

If you can't watch it, here's the gist:

The creative has just been pitched to the client, and the client immediately comes in with an objection.

To counter, Don Draper concludes the meeting, forcing the

client to either accept his expertise or walk out the door.

In *Pitch Anything*[7], Oren Klaff calls this the 'Prize frame'. Don knows the value he brings. Instead of Don feeling like he has to convince the client to work with him, it's the clients that have to convince Don that they aren't wasting his time.

The client must win you over, which is the opposite of what's happening in most coaching relationships...

We spend our time and energy convincing our clients to work with us. And so it's no wonder that respect, value, and desire diminish quickly.

Not only are we making it too easy for our clients, but we're also making them the prize!

Of course, the way you do this is key...

It shouldn't be done in an obnoxious or manipulative way. Rather, in a way that encourages your client to step up and get out of their own way so they can make a good business decision.

If you're truly honest with yourself, you know there's little value in trying to convince someone to work with you that doesn't believe in the work you are doing. So it's up to you to value yourself and your work, to protect yourself and your team from taking on a troublesome client.

One of my favourite questions to ask in the sales process is "What gives you a sense that you're a good fit for [insert coaching program]"

Don't make the mistake of thinking this is just a selling technique. Create an element of 'the chase' throughout your work, too.

We know that respect and value diminish as soon as people get what they want, so your client should never feel like they completely own you.

Dangle in front of them what is unattainable.

Play to their desire.

You are the prize. You are the talent. You are the greener grass.

Personal Reflection:

- Do I believe that I am the prize?
- Do I agree that my clients can't be truly successful without my help, guidance, and support?
- What do I need to do differently from today so that my clients have to convince me to work with them?

4

LIKED VS RESPECTED?

"If you set out to be liked, you would be prepared to compromise on anything at any time, and you would achieve nothing."

MARGARET THATCHER

At 3 am on 14th June 2019, I gave up alcohol.

I'm proud to say that I have not had a single drop since. I haven't given in to the peer pressure from my friends, family, and our prominent alcohol culture.

I go to bed relatively early, I don't go to pubs, I don't stay late at parties, I don't get drunk with my friends, and I don't lose days to hangovers and sickness.

Have I missed out on some experiences? Do people miss me in these situations? Have I let people down? Have I lost some friends? Have I grown apart from others? Do some people not like me as much any more?

Yes, all of these things are true.

I'm not looking for a pat on the back, but it's interesting to understand how I've tackled this.

I have been able to remain sober because I'm clear on my purpose, and what I want for myself, and I'm not willing to let other people or influences carry me away from my own values and principles.

The daily decision to not drink comes back to the respect I have for myself.

If I want people to like me, all I have to do is one simple thing...

Take a drink.

Back in 2022, on my three-year anniversary, a close friend said to me "I'm now starting to understand and respect your sobriety."

If you want to earn the respect of others, you have to respect yourself first — if you don't, how can you expect others to ever respect you?

And so, should we strive to be liked or to earn respect?

We must recognise and understand that the need to be liked comes from other people's perception of us, which we do not control, and earning respect starts from within us, which we have complete control over.

This is the foundation for where it all starts, and where it can all fall apart.

The need to be liked leads to agreeableness, compromise, ignorance, slow decision-making, and the impossible task of trying to please everyone.

Leading with the need to be liked breeds mediocre outcomes and results, and we're not interested in that.

We tend to respect people who are confident and competent in their areas of expertise. People with a clear sense of purpose, clear boundaries and expectations, who are consistent in their behaviour.

They expect more from themselves and from those around them, and they care about doing the right thing, even if it's not popular.

You know where you stand with them, and you don't get the sense that they are pretending to be someone other than themselves.

Ask yourself: Can I be both?

I'd be lying to you if I said that it wasn't important for me to feel liked and connected to the people I spend the most time with — my friends and family, my clients, and my peers.

Also, people tend to want to work with people they like. But as a coach or leader, your 'likeability' on its own isn't going to bring out the very best in people.

And so, the truth for most of us is that it's important to be liked AND respected.

But we need to get them in the right order.

Striving to be liked first comes with the risk of not being respected ever.

You don't need to be liked to be respected, but being respected first increases your chances of being liked later.

Personal Reflection:

- In what way is my need to be liked diminishing my authority with my clients?
- What something I hold back on saying because my client might not like me?
- How is my need to be liked holding my clients back from being successful at their highest potential?

5

BEING 'RADICALLY CANDID' - PART I

"The key is that Challenging Directly and showing you Care Personally are both sensitive to context and perception; they get measured at the listener's ear, not at the speaker's mouth."

KIM SCOTT

Our job as coaches is to say what we see.

But most managers and professionals can't do this because they are far too agreeable and 'nice.' They don't say what they really want and need to say.

They filter it; they dilute it.

Don't get me wrong, this doesn't mean we get a license to be obnoxious assholes — we have to work hard to find the balance between being direct, and showing that we care.

The best framework that helps Authoritative Coaches to strike that perfect balance is Kim Scott's Radical Candor[8].

Having taught Radical Candor to literally 100s of professionals, I have seen first-hand the dramatic shift it has on their approach to their communication, and ultimately the value they bring to their work.

The philosophy has become foundational to the way I communicate and is ultimately a big part of the value I bring to my work — the ability to be clear, direct, and step into conversations where others are unwilling. In fact, often times I'm the only person that can say what needs to be said.

And it's not just about learning to communicate better, it's about your mindset and approach to your work with your clients.

Radical Candor sets the tone and foundation for what it means to be an authoritative communicator, and ultimately a great coach, leader, and manager.

It will help you:

- See the true value of clear and direct communication ***(it's worth it)***
- Feel more confident about being clear and direct ***(you can be that person)***
- Get over the need to be liked and build the respect people have for you ***(is it more important to be liked, or respected?)***
- Get over your own difficult feelings ***(it's not about you)***

- Shift from 'friend' to 'expert/professional' ***(increase your value)***
- Be more consistent ***(people know who you are with them)***
- Be the person people go to when they want honest feedback ***(you do the right thing)***
- Teach others to communicate better ***(you show it, and you can teach it)***

Like most things, it's not valuable just as a theory...it needs to be put to work. The key to success with Radical Candor is finding opportunities to practice it in real-life situations, and as you become more self-aware, you will find opportunities to be more radically candid with the people you work with.

I guarantee you that if you do this one thing, and practice it deliberately, it will make a dramatic shift in the value you bring to your work.

Next, let's look at the framework from a coaching perspective.

Personal Reflection:

- As an Authoritative Coach, do I accept that I am likely to be the only person that can say what needs to be said?
- Can you see the link between being more direct and being more valuable as an Authoritative Coach?
- Do you believe that it's possible to be direct and authoritative without being an asshole?

6

BEING 'RADICALLY CANDID' - PART II

"The single biggest problem in communication is the illusion that it has taken place."

GEORGE BERNARD SHAW

What would you do if you saw that a client of yours had spinach in their teeth, directly before delivering a critical sales pitch to a prospective buyer?

According to Kim Scott's Radical Candor framework, there are 4 ways you could approach this.

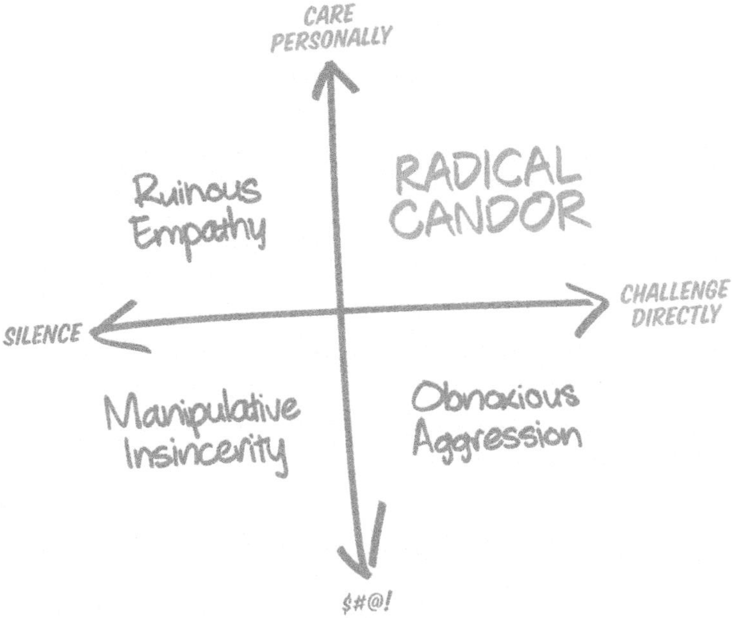

Radical Candor Framework, by Kim Scott[9]

Obnoxious Aggression: In front of the whole team you shout: "Allan! You've got spinach in your teeth! Didn't you check!? Don't you know how important this is! Go and sort yourself out!"

Manipulative Insincerity: Gossiping behind his back you whisper: "Look at Allan! Did you see that he has spinach in his teeth? Honestly, he's such an idiot. I hope he screws up this pitch and embarrasses himself."

Ruinous Empathy: You see the spinach, but it's too awkward and embarrassing for you to say anything, so you sit there in silence and let Allan go through with the pitch. Afterwards,

Allan approaches you: "Chris, why didn't you tell me I had spinach in my teeth, I thought you were my friend?!"

Radical Candor: You take Allan to the side inconspicuously and say to him, "Allan, you've got spinach in your teeth. I thought you should know. Let's nail this pitch!"

80% of the 100s of professionals I have worked with tend to gravitate towards ruinous empathy in difficult and awkward situations like this — and they didn't realise this until they got familiar with the Radical Candor framework and they could finally place a label on it!

The need to be liked keeps you ruinously empathetic. Yes, candor takes courage, and it can be difficult and awkward, but we all know that it's for the best to be more direct.

We're all great 'fair weather' communicators

Now, generally speaking, when things are going smoothly and to plan, there's nothing obviously wrong with the way we communicate. We can all be decent 'fair weather' communicators. It's when things get even just a little more difficult we start to clearly see the gaps in our communication.

And so, having read through these different approaches to the spinach scenario above, and with reference to the framework, how would you say you communicate when things get difficult?

Think about these 7 common coaching scenarios:

1. Providing direct and critical feedback to a client about their quality of work.
2. Helping a client see that a particular behaviour is getting in their way of doing their best work.
3. Someone screwed up but doesn't know it.
4. A client is showing up in a way that's negatively impacting the work and the relationship.
5. A client isn't doing the most important work and is wasting everyone's time.
6. A client is continually late to meetings or missing deadlines.
7. You have to fire a client.

Kim Scott gives us a framework to help us communicate in a radically candid way. If you treat the Radical Candor framework as a compass — to direct your conversations towards the top right of the quadrants, you can strike the balance that shows you care personally while being direct and clear.

Here are a few pointers to get you moving towards radical candor with direct and critical feedback:

- Communicate immediately while it's relevant and helpful. Don't hold on to it until 'the right time'.
- Do it in person. Don't try to make it easier for yourself by doing it by email or direct message — this almost never works out well.
- Do it privately. Don't do it in front of peers, colleagues or subordinates.
- Make sure it's specific to the behaviour or the task. Don't make it about their character or identity.

- Make it helpful so they know what to do next and what support looks like.

Furthermore, if you can step into situations like this and remember that it's not about you, and that you could be wrong, that will help you start with the right mindset and in the right place.

Just imagine how you'd feel if your 'friends' at work knew you were walking around with spinach in your teeth — but no one told you.

Don't forget: Clear is kind.

Personal Reflection:

- When I'm under pressure or when I can't confidently address a situation with a client, do I gravitate toward Ruinous Empathy or Obnoxious Aggression?
- In what way does that diminish my ability to be an Authoritative Coach with my clients?
- What's a recent client scenario where I could have been more 'radically candid'? What would that have looked like? How would it have led to a better outcome?
- What's a current client issue that I'm avoiding, and I know if I don't deal with it it'll lead to bigger problems later?

II

STATUS

The stakes are highest when you first meet your client. You don't get a second chance to make a great first impression. You're going to do everything within your control to ensure they are the right fit. You will define the coach-client relationship, manage their expectations, and position yourself as an authority so the client gets a sense of who's in control and leading the way. What happens next will set the tone for what it's like to work with an Authoritative Coach.

7

WHY NOW?

"Asking 'why now?' isn't just asking a question — it's asking everything."

EDITH EGER

One of the major mistakes we make in the sales process is spending all our time trying to convince a coaching prospect why they should become our client, and what we know to be true is that the more we try to convince, the more we diminish our authority.

What's far more powerful is to ask questions that put your prospects on their heels so they have to prove why they are a good fit for you.

A key question to add to your initial calls with prospective clients is:

"What gives you a sense that you are a good fit for [insert coaching program]?"

Add "Why now?", and you've got yourself a powerful combination of questions that gives your client a clear sense of what this relationship is going to look like, how different it will be from what they are used to, and ultimately setting up the foundations for a strong coach-client relationship.

Edith Eger expresses the power of this short question in her book, The Choice[10]:

"'Why now?' I asked. This was my secret weapon. The question I always ask my patients on a first visit. I need to know why they are motivated to change. Why today, of all days, do they want to start working with me? Why is today different from yesterday, or last week, or last year? Why is today different from tomorrow? Sometimes our pain pushes us, and sometimes our hope pulls us."

Use these questions to show your clients what a true authoritative coaching experience looks like from the very beginning of your relationship.

8

THE RELATIONSHIP

"Don't tell me the moon is shining; show me the glint of light on broken glass."

ANTON CHEKHOV

One of the most important aspects that will determine the success of your work as a coach is the strength of the relationship you have with your client.

I know clearly the times when we haven't achieved together what we set out to do, it was almost always due to some kind of breakdown in the relationship. I know that I could have done more to manage expectations and establish what our relationship should look like from the beginning.

I'm not a big believer in 'you don't get a second chance to make a first impression' because there are almost always second and even third chances.

However, this is one of those rare occasions where if you don't do the work at the beginning of the relationship, it's impossible to claw it back — and so it becomes critical to do deliberate work on the client relationship at the beginning.

Here's an example of the coaching questions I will use when setting the conditions for a new client relationship:

- What does our relationship need to look like in order to do our best work?
- What do you feel contributes to a healthy coach/client relationship?
- Have you ever hired a coach or consultant before? What went well/not so well? or What was helpful/unhelpful?

Of course, it's important that you have a good idea of what kind of answers you are looking for so you can manage expectations.

A healthy discussion on this topic with your client will create better alignment, and clearer expectations, and even give you permission to be the best coach you can be.

Many years ago I remember asking a new client what our relationship should look like, and here's what she said:

> ***"In my past experience, the best relationships I've had with [coaches] have been the ones that aren't afraid to push, that want to push their clients to be better. Nothing makes me feel more frustrated than when I feel like I'm pushing a [coach] along. I want to feel like a [coach] is***

> ***challenging me."***

In this example, she gave me clear permission to challenge her, which of course is a big component of being the best coach I can be.

Don't skip this discussion with your clients.

Take the time to establish what your relationship needs to look like. They will probably tell you everything you need to hear, and it'll lead to a truly great working relationship.

9

PROBLEMS

"No one saves us but ourselves. No one can and no one may. We ourselves must walk the path."

BUDDHA

When your client comes to you with a problem, they want you to sweep in and solve the problem for them, take away the pain, save them. In some cases, they even want you to take the blame, to take responsibility for the problem.

But, you wouldn't be doing your job if you did that.

You aren't here to rescue your client from their problems. No real learning takes place when you rescue people. Instead, shift from a rescuer to a coach[11] and use questions to not only delegate the problem back to them but to help them see the problem more clearly so they can work through it.

And so, when your client comes to you with a problem, you can ask:

"How have we allowed this to happen?"

or

"What factors have led to this problem?"

or

"How long are we willing to let this continue?"

Using these questions forces your client to work through the problem so they can uncover the root cause and land on a better solution.

When you help them get there for themselves they are more likely to own it, take responsibility, and do the work to solve it — and prevent it from happening again in the future.

What's a recent client situation where these questions would have helped you to delegate the problem back to the client, and ultimately respond like an Authoritative Coach?

10

ACCOUNTABILITY

"Responsibility equals accountability equals ownership. And a sense of ownership is the most powerful weapon a team or organization can have."

PAT SUMMITT

You're doing a good job as a coach if you are leaving your coaching sessions with nothing on your plate — with all work delegated to the client.

However, what can quickly happen is that you become an 'accountability partner' — in that you find yourself chasing down your clients for their work, making sure they're on track.

This is a huge waste of time, and I refuse to accept this as my reality as a coach.

Once the work has been agreed upon, here are a few key

coaching questions that will help you delegate accountability to your client:

- Out of these priorities, which one is the most important right now?
- What's an action you will be taking in the next 24 hours to move this forward?
- What's a potential challenge or roadblock that could prevent you from completing this priority?
- What does support look like from me?
- What do you want me to do if I see you getting off track?

...and to finish up, get an agreement that you expect them to let you know immediately if they are getting off track with their work.

Personal Reflection

- How much time and energy am I spending chasing people up for their work?
- How often do my clients miss deadlines?
- How long am I going to let this continue?

Use these questions to teach your clients how to own their own work.

11

RESPONSIBILITY

"We all create the person we become by our choices as we go through life. In a real sense, by the time we are adults, we are the sum total of the choices we have made."

ELEANOR ROOSEVELT

In chapter 1 we discussed the distinction between a consultant and a coach - that it's found in who's doing most of the thinking:

- When a client goes to their consultant with a problem, the consultant will do all the thinking, do the hard work, and present the client with a solution.
- When a client goes to their coach with a problem, the coach will guide the client through the problem, help them think through it, so they can own the solution for themselves.

Now, there's a suitable time for both methods, but arguably the coach provides more long-term value since they force the client to think critically, make better decisions and rely upon themselves to solve problems in the future.

The challenge for the coach is to not default to 'consultant' mode and immediately provide advice and solutions, and to slow down to help their client learn that this is not what a coach does.

And so, when a client comes to me with a problem, I'm not going to allow them to outsource the hard part — making the decision, developing the plan, coming up with the solution — to me. I will use variations of the following questions:

- "What do you think you should do?"
- "What are you going to do next?"

By asking these questions I put the responsibility back on to the client and over time the client learns to think for themselves. I want them to come to me with problems, and I want them to know I'm here to help, but I'm not going to take ownership of the problem.

As a coach, ask yourself:

- Who's doing all the thinking?
- Who's doing all the work?

...and next time your client comes to you with a problem, use these questions to guide them to solve it for themselves.

Contributed by Zach Basner[12]

12

COMPASSION

"Compassion is not a virtue — it is a commitment. It's not something we have or don't have — it's something we choose to practice."

BRENÉ BROWN

There are many attributes that make a coach a great coach. Two traits that can be somewhat controversial are: a) never being completely satisfied, and b) being highly sensitive to the mistakes our clients are making.

There's no question in my mind that these behaviours help us to be highly effective and valuable coaches.

However, it comes at the risk of losing our ability to show genuine compassion for the work and progress that the client is making.

What I've found in my work is that most clients quickly default to telling you what they aren't doing well versus spending time on what they are doing well, and there are two ways to bring more compassion into our work with our clients:

- The coach is able to explicitly and specifically state what is going well
- The coach brings it out of the client by leading with questions

The coach states what good looks like...

Whether or not the client is able to see the progress on their own, there's real value in spending time sharing explicitly with your client what you see as progress and great work.

It's healthy to assume that your client needs to hear this from you since you have relative experience — having been through this many times with your other clients.

It's the job of the coach to be the client's champion.

The coach brings it out of their clients...

If you get a sense that your client generally struggles to recognise their own work and their own progress, you can use this as an opportunity to 'train' your client to bring 'self-compassion' to their work, and you can do that by asking some key questions:

- What do you feel we have done well [insert time period]?
- What has been our single greatest achievement [insert time

period]?
- What does progress look like in [insert specific area of work]?
- What has been your greatest personal lesson?

You'll find with some clients that you have to be firm with them to make sure they stay in this place as they tend to quickly drift into what they aren't doing well, and here's a statement I use to help them stay in the right place:

"We're going to spend time today on what we want to do differently or better going forward, and before we do that, I'd like to hear from each of you - what do you feel has been our single greatest achievement in the last 3 months?"

What could you do differently or better with your clients to bring more compassion to the work you are doing together?

Personal Reflection

- What specifically are my clients doing well right now? When was the last time I told them?
- In what situations do my clients tend to gravitate towards the negative?

13

BLAME

"The manager who comes up with the right solution to the wrong problem is more dangerous than the manager who comes up with the wrong solution to the right problem."

PETER DRUCKER

In our work with clients, things are going to go wrong.

Projects will take longer.

Results won't meet expectations.

Clients will get upset and frustrated.

It's inevitable, so we better get good at working with our clients when issues arise.

What I see in the coaching world is that all too often we fall on our own sword when we're presented with a problem. We apologise, immediately take the blame, and dive head first into solving the problem.

This is not always a helpful response because it hinders our ability to respond objectively to the problem and ask the right questions.

The skills that increase our value to our clients is our ability to make sure we are:

- Working on the right problems
- Doing the work in the right order
- Not making stupid mistakes
- Many steps ahead and preventing future problems

What our clients really need from us is not to take the blame, but to help them through solving the problem.

They are coming to us because they need help from an expert.

So, don't be so quick to take the blame. Instead, rise above it. See the difficulty the client is having dealing with the problem, and figure out if you're actually working on the right problem.

When problems occur in my work with clients, the type of coaching questions I ask are:

- When did you first realise this was a problem?
- Why am I only finding out now?
- What do you think has caused the problem?
- How have we allowed this to happen?

- What have we done to try and fix the problem?
- What do you think we're missing?
- How important is this compared to everything else we're working on right now?
- What kind of impact is this having on the business?

And so, next time your client comes to you with a problem that would normally have you falling on your own sword or jumping into action, slow down, think objectively, ask better questions, and increase your value to your clients.

III

WORK

You can't predict everything that's going to arise in the day-to-day of coaching. That's what keeps the work interesting! In the following short and practical chapters you will find various tried and tested coaching scenarios to give you a sense of how to respond authoritatively to real-life client situations. As you expose yourself to unfamiliar coaching territory, come back to these chapters often and role-play the scenarios so that when they do eventually come up, you're ready.

14

THE VALUE OF COACHING

"When people express opinions that differ from yours, take it as a chance to grow. Seek to understand over being understood. Be curious, not defensive. The only way to disarm another human being is by listening."

GLENNON DOYLE

In more recent years, the focus of my work has been coaching and training leaders who want to become certified They Ask, You Answer coaches — in other words, the coaching of coaches.

I've been teaching them what I've learned over the past 10 years or so, and my mission is to get them there faster and in a better state by making sure they learn from my own mistakes. (And I've made a lot of them!)

One of the coaching skills I've tested hard for is the ability of a coach to respond well in difficult moments.

- A client comes to you with a problem: "We're spending all this money, and we're not seeing results..."
- A client is frustrated with your coaching: "I'm paying you to help solve these problems, and all you do is ask questions!"
- A client wants to quit: "This isn't working for us, and we want to cancel."

In initial role-plays, what typically happens is that the coach will take it personally, try to defend their situation, and justify their value. Worst case, they blame it on the client. Almost always, the coach buckles under the pressure from the client. As you can imagine, this doesn't end up in a good place.

What we're looking for is a response that sounds something like: "I'm pleased you're bringing this to me, this is exactly what you and I should be talking about..."

We reframe conflict as a problem and see it as an opportunity to strengthen and galvanise our relationship with our client.

Sure, the client is frustrated, angry, and emotional, but that's what makes you valuable to them.

In most circumstances, what the client really wants is your help to solve the problem with them. It's not personal, and what they need is an objective and rational person to help them through it.

Be the coach they need in order to help them get clear on what the real problem is. Believe in the power and value of coaching, and don't buckle under the pressure to be anything other than the best coach you can be.

As an Authoritative Coach you welcome your client problems, because you know you're the right person to be talking it through with. In the next chapter we'll look at exactly what to say when problems arise.

15

WHAT MAKES YOU SAY THAT?

"Every time you use 'yes, and' in a negative situation it steers the conversation in a positive direction."

VINH QUANG GIANG

In the previous section I discussed our ability to respond well to problems and difficult questions that our clients bring to the table.

We need to train ourselves to quickly respond to problems in a way that moves the conversation forward — what they call a 'yes, and...' in improv circles.

To change our mindset so we can see problems as opportunities. From feeling threatened and responding defensively, to being ready and open to the problem your client is bringing to you.

That's the mindset shift we're looking for, but what are we supposed to say next?

Through role-playing I help coaches to improve their ability to respond to unplanned moments in client conversations, and the question we keep coming back to is:

"What makes you say that?"

What I love about this is that it's genuinely curious, it stops us from making assumptions, it's non-judgmental, and it helps us to understand what's going on for the client.

Examples:

"We can't publish pricing information on our website." **What makes you say that?**

"As a sales leader, I don't need to be involved in this project." **What makes you say that?**

"We don't need to hire a content manager." **What makes you say that?**

"Our website isn't performing well." **What makes you say that?**

"We don't need a coach, we can do this on our own." **What makes you say that?**

You might look a little crazy to anyone that's with you right now, but take a moment to repeat the phrase over and over out loud right now and make it part of your vocabulary.

16

SAY WHAT YOU SEE

"It's my job to notice things and then say what I noticed."

JERRY SALTZ

As I've grown as a coach, I've become more invested in the success of my clients. What I mean by that is that I care so much about their growth that I can't sit back and watch them fail. I have to say something.

It's one of the major factors that motivates me to get over myself and be direct and clear.

It's when things get tough that we know if we're as good as we think we are — and, as you know, it's not always plain sailing with our clients. There are times when we have to deliberately bring up a difficult conversation that shines a light on a behaviour that's getting in their way.

Recently, one of my clients was trying to do too much, and

as a result, they weren't doing anything well. The Managing Director was getting stressed out about it, and ultimately there was a lot of tension in the room.

I could see it. It was obvious to me. And that's a lot of the value we bring as coaches — it's enough just not being in the day-to-day of your client's business to see what's really going on and bring value.

At that moment, the question I asked was:

"What's one thing that we're doing right now that you'd agree we're doing at our highest potential?"

Sure, it's a loaded question, but it was more important that they agreed that they were doing nothing well, and trying to do too much.

You might be thinking to yourself that this is a risky question, and it is. There's a chance the client could respond defensively to a question like this.

One thing we don't talk about often enough is how important the coach-client relationship is in terms of what questions we can ask. In this case, I have a strong bond with the client, which allowed me to bring this conversation up.

Our job as Authoritative Coaches is to manage and be comfortable with the tension between knowing that we're making progress, and at the same time knowing that we could be doing a lot better, and it can be tricky to get it right.

It's up to us to bring out the potential in others and help our clients get out of their own way by identifying limiting behaviours, and in order to do that, sometimes we have to put the brakes on.

Ask yourself: what's the obvious behaviour that's holding your clients back? Whose responsibility is it to shine a light on it? What's holding you back from saying what you see?

17

ENABLE

"We only see what we want to see; We only hear what we want to hear. Our belief system is just like a mirror that only shows us what we believe."

DON MIGUEL RUIZ

The questions we ask act as a mirror for our clients. It forces them to look at themselves from a different perspective.

More often than not, the reason our clients aren't moving at the pace we'd like them to is because they are getting in their own way.

Instead of telling them why, we use questions to get them to articulate it for themselves.

What we know is that if the client discovers the problem for themselves, they are more likely to own it, change their behaviour, and ultimately do the work.

And so the questions we use in this situation are:

- What's holding us back [from doing this work]?
- What impact is this having on our progress?
- How long are we prepared to let this continue?

And you can wrap it up by asking: "So, what are you going to do about it?" or "What needs to change so we can do this work?"

Being external to the client's organisation is a big part of the value you bring. It allows you to see clearly and objectively what's holding them back and ultimately enable them to make progress.

It's your job as an Authoritative Coach to hold up the metaphorical mirror and help your clients see it for themselves.

18

EMPOWER

"The smartest person in the room is never as smart as all the people in the room."

JOHN C. MAXWELL

Being an authoritative coach overlaps heavily with being a great leader of people, and being a great leader means:

- You don't feel the need to be the smartest person in the room
- You don't make it about yourself
- You use your skills to elevate other people

Here's a quick and effective way to allow your clients to bring their ideas and solutions to the table.

Start the conversation by saying "I have a few ideas of my own, but I'd like to hear yours first..."

This way, you empower your clients to share their thoughts.

What ends up happening is that your clients come up with the solutions you had in mind, but the difference between them coming up with it themselves versus you telling them what to do is dramatically different: They will be more invested in the process and the results.

And when they come up with the same, and often times better ideas than yours, you allow them to have that moment. You're not threatened by other people's smart ideas, and you don't make it about you.

Next time you are collaborating with your clients, go last and see what happens.

19

WHAT IF I'M WRONG?

"Don't make assumptions. Find the courage to ask questions...communicate with others as clearly as you can to avoid misunderstandings."

DON MIGUEL RUIZ

A few years ago I came in hot with an opinion about why a new idea was a bad idea.

I was cocky, arrogant, and obnoxious about it, which is unlike me, but for some reason I thought this was the right approach to make sure people listened to me... and, of course, it turned out to be a terrible approach.

- There was no seeking to understand
- There was no humility or humbleness in finding out if this idea might actually work
- There was no elevating of other people
- There was no effort to collaborate and build upon the idea

And that's when my coach and mentor said to me:

"What you've missed here is that you could be wrong."

I learned this lesson the hard way, and I now use this as a filter to help me communicate better.

Knowing that you could be wrong is a powerful position to come from. It stops you from making a fool of yourself, puts you in a better place to work and collaborate with others, and it forces you to seek to understand first before jumping to conclusions and making assumptions.

Try asking yourself "what if I'm wrong?" before jumping in with your opinion, and see how it changes your approach as an Authoritative Coach.

20

REFRAME

"If you don't like something, change it; if you can't change it, change the way you think about it."

MARY ENGELBREIT

When our clients come to us for help, they are often stuck in their way of thinking.

They have made assumptions, told themselves a story, and run with a narrative so they can't see any other possibilities.

As a result, they hold themselves back from making decisions, moving forward, and ultimately growing as a person.

As an Authoritative Coach, it's your job to focus on the person and help them see how they are getting in their own way.

We have to help them without making them feel like they are

wrong.

We use questions to help them to reframe the way they are thinking.

Here are the two key phrases you can use to help reframe a client's way of thinking:

1. Is it possible...
2. What if you knew that...

Here's an example...

Let's say a client comes to you because a colleague lied to them about something important. They are angry, frustrated, and they don't know if they can trust them again.

Even though this is their truth, you know that you have to challenge their perspective.

To do it well, you are going to focus on the person rather than the story — how they are dealing with the situation rather than how the situation came to be.

Your coaching questions would look something like:

1. Is it possible...that they didn't lie to you at all?
2. What if you knew that...they simply changed their mind and haven't gotten around to telling you yet?

Of course, timing is everything. When helping someone reframe their thinking, you don't want to ask questions like this too early when they aren't ready for it.

And so, when you are having high-stakes conversations with your clients and team members, ask yourself:

- How is this way of thinking/behaviour holding them back?
- How can I help them see the same situation from a different perspective?

As Authoritative Coaches, this how we deepen our relationships with the people we work with - by shining a light on the things they can't see for themselves.

21

PERSON VS STORY - PART I

"You know, if you know the answer, but you don't know the question you are in a bad way. But if you have questions, you will find answers."

SALVADOR MINUCHIN

Let's say your client comes to you because they are getting resistance internally from their team about the work you are doing together, and they are finding it difficult to confidently deal with these questions and objections.

You have a number of options in terms of where to coach from. Let's take a look at them:

Coaching in the story

Who said what? What did you say? Why don't they get it? Why is it a problem that they don't get it? What should they be saying? How should they be behaving?

The coach is distracted by getting information from the client that only serves the interests of the coach. It doesn't help the client.

Coaching for results

Why did we decide to do this work? Why do you think it's valuable? How are other people holding us back? How do we get them to buy in? Why don't they get it?

The coach is worried that other people are going to hold the client back from getting the results we have to achieve from our work together, which distracts us from getting to the real problem.

Coaching the person

What is making it difficult for you to respond to these people in the moment? How is this holding you back from growing in your role? If you could respond more confidently, what kind of impact would this have for you?

The coach is able to cut through the noise and see the real challenge that the person is having, thus coaching the person in the place that's going to make the biggest impact for them, and by extension, the results from the work we're doing together.

The key question in this scenario is "what is making it difficult for you to respond in the moment?" because it focuses the coaching on the person and where they need help.

As Authoritative Coaches, these challenges are unique opportunities to galvanise our relationship with the people that we are working with.

Every challenge brings an opportunity to coach the person.

Don't get distracted by the story.

22

PERSON VS STORY - PART II

"The player of the inner game comes to value the art of relaxed concentration above all other skills; he discovers a true basis for self-confidence; and he learns that the secret to winning any game lies in not trying too hard."

W. TIMOTHY GALLWEY

A question I get asked a lot is "how do you know what question to ask?" — as if there's some kind of script or plan.

The answer isn't what people want to hear.

Often times I don't know what question I'm going to ask.

And this is what's getting in the way of people becoming truly effective coaches.

They might be too busy worrying about what they need to say

that they aren't focusing on where the right questions are more likely to come from.

And where is that?

You will know what to ask if you are truly focused on the person right in front of you.

In the Inner Game of Tennis[13], Timothy Gallwey talks about helping tennis players get into their flow by focusing on the seam of the tennis ball:

"This time I want you to focus your mind on the seams of the ball. Don't think about making contact. In fact, don't try to hit the ball at all. Just let your racket contact the ball where it wants, and we'll see what happens."

To translate the metaphor to our work with people — the 'seams of the ball' are the words, the body language, the tone, and the behaviour of the person we are communicating with.

Focus on the person; stay in the moment

Our work here is to eliminate all distractions in our mind so we can have a total and complete focus on the person right in front of us.

The question I often ask myself when I'm focusing on the person I'm coaching is:

"Why are they sharing this with me?"

The questions Authoritative Coaches ask are not part of a plan or a script; what we ask next is a response generated from total and complete focus on the person.

So I encourage you to let go of the pressure to always have the next question ready and, instead, simply let it happen.

Say to yourself:

- Why is this difficult for them?
- Why are they sharing this with me?

23

DISARM

"Seek first to understand, then to be understood."

STEPHEN COVEY

The above quote is well known as the 5th habit from the perennial 7 Habits of Highly Effective People[14] by Stephen Covey.

However, just because it's well known, doesn't mean it's well executed!

Let me give you an example:

Let's say you've just attended a client meeting where one of your peers, Dave, undermined your value in front of the client. It's not the first time it's happened, and now you're frustrated and angry about it.

You decide that you are going to do something about it, and

so in the heat of the moment you walk into Dave's office and challenge him.

It goes something like this:

You: "I'm getting completely fed up with you speaking about me in front of clients like that; it makes me look stupid!"

Of course, Dave has no idea what you're talking about and immediately defends himself from the attack:

Dave: "What do you mean? I've got no idea what you're talking about! Don't come in here and start accusing me!"

This is often how conversations start — attack, defend — no sign of anyone seeking to understand.

Everyone is armed and ready to fight.

What would it look like if we led with seeking to understand first?

You: "Dave, Can you help me with something? In the meeting we just had with [CLIENT] you said [INSERT STATEMENT], could you help me understand what you meant by that?"

Dave: "Sure, what I meant was..."

Do you see how the difference?

When we seek first to understand, we avoid making assumptions (in this case, we're disproving our assumptions). We start the conversation in a better place instead of jumping ahead, and it disarms the situation so we can have a better and more rational conversation.

It's our job as an Authoritative Coach to set the conditions for better and more transformative conversations to take place.

And so, your go-to coaching phrases for your toolbox are...:

1. Can you help me with something...?
2. Could you help me understand...?

...so your clients lean into you, instead of fighting against you.

24

WHAT VS WHY

“A ‘what’ question becomes incredibly powerful when it forces the client to think about something in a new way, rather than tell you something they already know.”

MARION FRANKLIN

Ideally, we want every question we ask to feel like we’re making PROGRESS, that the question has PURPOSE, and it leads us to the PRIORITY (what’s important).

This is called The 3 Ps of Questioning.

What we’re trying to stay away from is the other person a) feeling like it’s an interrogation, or b) getting frustrated because the conversation isn’t moving forward and feels useless.

And so, just because we know we should be asking questions as coaches, doesn’t give us a license to ask as many questions as we want. Perhaps more importantly, we should be obsessed with asking better questions.

I'd like to revisit Marion Franklin's The HeART of Laser-Focused Coaching[15] and pull an example from the book where she looks at why 'what' questions are generally better coaching questions compared to using why and how questions.

Why vs How vs What...

Now, imagine your client has booked and paid to attend an upcoming business conference and we can choose between three different types of questions:

1. Why did you choose this conference?

- Responses will likely begin with "because..."
- Looks to the past
- Appears judgmental
- Asks the client to justify their decision

2. How did you choose this conference?

- Client describes the factors that helped them choose
- Doesn't move the conversation forward (still in the past)
- A 'how' question is better at the end of a coaching conversation (about how you will accomplish something)

3. What do you expect to gain from this conference?

- Provides more relevant data
- Allows you to go deeper based on what the client discloses

- Looks to the future instead of the past

As a coach you probably aren't going to use 'what' questions 100% of the time, but just reading this note should have you increasing the percentage of 'what' questions, especially if you can turn your attention to turning 'why' and 'how' questions into 'what' questions.

Finally, ask yourself 'who's doing all the thinking?' - is it you, or the client? As a coach, if you're doing all the thinking, you're not asking the right questions, and as a result, your client won't grow.

Challenge yourself to rephrase your questions and report back on how that helps you to be a more Authoritative Coach.

25

ASK WHY TO VERIFY

"Trust, but verify."

RONALD REAGAN

How often do we make the assumption that what has been said has been fully and clearly understood?

As much as we trust our clients, it's critical that we never skip the step of verifying their understanding from their perspective. We trust and verify.

The way this shows up in my coaching and training is by asking variations of 'Why is it important that we do it this way?'

Or simply, 'why?'

This question is important for a few reasons:

First, it forces the client to articulate it for themselves, and in order to do that, they have to think for themselves.

Second, it gives me an opportunity to dial up the importance of the work by digging deeper. (What kind of problem does this solve for? What impact does it have? What would be a reason why we would stop doing this? How important is it that we never skip this?)

Third, before we move on to the next topic or lesson, I can quickly get a sense of any gaps in their knowledge and respond accordingly, making sure that I haven't made assumptions.

Finally, if the client can say it back to me in a clear way, it gives me the confidence that not only have they learned and understood it, but they have also internalised and therefore own it for themselves.

What we don't want to have happen is that the client keeps making the same mistakes, or missing out on important steps, and we waste a lot of time going back over the same ground.

So, what we do is build time into our coaching work to verify that the client has got this and we're moving forward with the work we're doing together.

Where can you use this question in your work with your clients?

Contributed by Brian Casey[16]

26

SHORTER QUESTIONS

"I begin to speak only when I'm certain what I'll say isn't better left unsaid."

CATO

One of the challenges coaches-in-training must overcome is asking long, rambling questions.

When the coach does more of the talking, it slows the pace of the conversation, and the client gets frustrated, bored, and tunes out.

Worse, you diminish your authority. You look like you don't know what you're doing, and the client begins to question the value you bring.

We don't want this, so why do we do it?

We believe that asking a question, without explaining why, is rude, disrespectful, or bullish.

We are afraid of pissing people off.

And we overcome that fear by justifying what we are about to ask — we 'run up' to the question.

We make it about ourselves, rather than the client.

The thing is, many of us have spent a lifetime having to explain ourselves to people.

It's become a habit. That habit stops today.

You do not need to continually justify or explain yourself.

Ironically, it's the long rambling questions that are more likely to piss your client off.

Ask yourself: What is the shortest possible question that moves the conversation forward and maintains a sense of purpose?

Here's a list of short questions and phrases to add to your coaching toolbox:

- Be more specific...
- Why is that a problem?
- What's the problem with that?
- What's the real problem?
- What do you want?
- What else?

- Say more...
- You're frustrated, why?
- Why not?
- What's changed?
- Why now?
- Why?
- What makes you say that?
- What's next?

Shorter questions are specific, punchy, clear, and hard to avoid.

Shorter questions increase your authority and make you a better coach.

As ever, it's over to you now to work on your self-awareness to catch yourself when you are justifying your question — bite your tongue, and ask a shorter question.

Report back on the difference it makes to your coaching conversations.

27

MISTAKES

"All men make mistakes, but only wise men learn from their mistakes."

WINSTON CHURCHILL

In The Death of Expertise[17], Tom Nichols shares:

"An expert is someone who knows some of the worst mistakes that can be made in his subject and how to avoid them." - Werner Heisenberg

And

"An expert is someone who has made all the mistakes which can be made in a very narrow field." - Niels Bohr

A big part of the value you bring to your clients and to your work is the fact that you've been around long enough to know what not to do.

As you are probably aware by now, a big part of my coaching style and philosophy is to empower my clients to make their own decisions, instead of telling them what to do (which is consulting, not coaching).

I do believe that there are some allowable mistakes that your clients have to make in order for them to learn and grow.

However, this has to be tempered with the fact that they are hiring you to help them avoid the most common mistakes so they can get there faster and in a better state than someone who is trying to do it on their own without a coach.

So, how can you simultaneously empower your clients, create self-discovery, lead with genuine curiosity and somehow help your clients avoid the most common mistakes?

The coaching statements or phrases that I find to be useful are:

- "What we don't want to have happen is..."
- "What history has shown us is..."
- "In my experience, what I've found to be true is..."

And if you believe they could self-discover the problems:

- "What could cause us to fail here?"
- "What problems may hold us back from being successful?"

In other words, the value we bring is the fact that we are always many steps ahead of our clients at all times and, based on our experience, we can predict what could go wrong.

We don't drop our empowering coaching style, but we do help them see what could happen if we go down this road. We can now let them use this new information to make better and more informed decisions, thus avoiding predictable and known mistakes.

Don't forget, as an Authoritative Coach you can't sit back and watch your client make mistakes that lead to failure. You must act.

28

MISUNDERSTANDINGS

"The overall purpose of human communication is - or should be - reconciliation. It should ultimately serve to lower or remove the walls of misunderstanding which unduly separate us human beings, one from another."

M. SCOTT PECK

I'd like to share a real-life example from my experience as a They Ask, You Answer coach to share a few key coaching questions with you.

In this scenario, the client has agreed that they want to be successful with They Ask, You Answer (a sales and marketing strategy and framework); we're doing the work, but early on in the process they come back to me and say something like:

"We've decided that we aren't going to publish any information about pricing on our website!"

Now, discussing pricing is a major element that impacts a client's ability to become the most trusted voice in their space.

Having worked through this example dozens of times, the biggest mistake the coach makes is immediately shifting into a pitch of why the client needs to discuss pricing on their website.

The coach reacts by shifting into an 'I'm right and you're wrong' type mindset, which almost always becomes a debate or an argument and doesn't lead to a good outcome or coaching experience.

The power of leading with questions...

Instead, what the coach needs to do is not make assumptions and shift to asking good questions.

The two key questions that help you respond better in a situation like this are:

- What's changed? Or, what led to this decision?
- What do you understand about how we should discuss pricing on our website in a 'They Ask, You Answer' way?

In turn, what we tend to find is that the client has simply misunderstood and is unclear about what they are supposed to be doing.

And so, our job as coaches is to not prove them wrong or make them feel like they are wrong, but instead assume that they've misunderstood and they're not clear, because if they did understand, they wouldn't be having this challenge.

As always, instead of trying to be right, let your curiosity lead you to a place of understanding.

29

SCOPE CREEP

"The essence of strategy is choosing what not to do."

MICHAEL PORTER

This question alone can eliminate scope creep, clarify conflicting priorities and prevent unmanageable workloads.

You can use it with clients, your boss, and even with yourself!

What I love about this question is that, if you use it in a genuine way, you aren't saying no — you are helping everyone, including yourself, to make sure we're doing the right work, and our best work.

Your boss comes to you with a new idea. You say:

"How does this new request stack up against everything else in terms of priority? What would you like me to de-prioritise in order to prioritise this?"

Your client comes to you with a new request. You say:

"Looking at the scope of the project, is this new request more of a priority than the work we've already agreed to?"

Someone comes to you with an opportunity. You ask yourself:

"If I say yes to this, what am I saying no to?"

Part of your job as an Authoritative Coach is to use variations of this question to act as a check to make sure your clients aren't getting distracted by blindly making choices to do whatever takes their fancy.

Instead, we make sure they are doing the the right work, in the right order, and they aren't doing anything that could risk their chance of success.

30

FOCUS

"When people are crystal clear about the most important priorities of the organization, not only are they many times more productive, they discover they have the time they need to have a whole life."

STEPHEN COVEY

This is a helpful question to have in your coaching toolbox when your client or team member is focusing on too many things or doesn't have clear priorities.

It's called 'The Focus Question'[18].

Use this when you want to get them to bring something critical into focus, and help them see that they have been ignoring something important.

The original question:

“What’s one thing you could start doing that, if you did on a regular basis, would make a tremendous positive difference in your personal life?”

A variation:

“What’s one thing you could start doing that, if you made it a priority, would make a tremendous positive difference to the results in your business?”

Your clients are easily distracted, and they often can’t see the woods for the trees. Fortunately, they’ve got you to lean on - being external to the organisation means you can see the woods *and* the trees. Use variations of this question to help your clients come up with better solutions to problems and focus on the specific actions they need to take.

31

WE'RE NOT DONE YET

"When you are reacting to the other person, that person owns the frame. When the other person is reacting to what you do and say, you own the frame."

OREN KLAFF

One of the challenges I used to have in my work as a They Ask, You Answer[19] coach, was that after a relatively short space of time clients would say things like:

- We're done now
- We've got it from here
- Looks like we've got everything we need
- We don't need to work with you and your team any more

There are a few reasons why this is a problem.

Firstly, it's really the coach that should be in the position to determine if we're done or not, not the client. After all, it's the coach that has done this work dozens of times and knows what true success looks like.

Secondly, as the coach, we know the work is not done, but it's difficult to convince the client they need to keep working with you if they've already come to that decision on their own.

So, what we need to do is get ahead of this problem to make sure it doesn't come up.

We start at the beginning. Let your client know that we are going to, as part of the process, facilitate a 90-day planning session so that we can review our work and strategically identify our key priorities for the next 90 days.

In that 90-day session, we start with a simple coaching question:

"Looking ahead over the next three months, what do you feel are your top three digital sales and marketing challenges?"

For each of the priorities we then ask these questions:

- On a scale of 1 to 10, how well would you say we're performing in this area right now?
- Are we OK with this?
- Where do we need to be?
- What does success look like?
- Let's assume we do everything right, how long will it take to get there?
- What's important for us to achieve over the next three

months?
- Who will be responsible for this work?

By the end of this process, you should have three clear priorities that are set out in a way that makes it easy to track over the next three months (Think: SMART goals[20]).

At IMPACT[21], we've taken this one step further and created an interactive scorecard tool[22] that allows our clients to score themselves from 1-100 on where they are right now. They can very clearly see two things: Firstly, that they have made progress, and secondly, and perhaps more importantly, there's still a lot of work to do.

Of course, the whole purpose is to make sure the client achieves success at their highest potential, and to have any chance of that being true we have to get ahead of the client getting in their own way by thinking they are done, when in fact they have got a lot more work to do.

It's over to you now — If you did something similar with your clients, would they stay with you for longer? Would they do the work that leads to true transformation?

32

NO 7s

"A ship is safe in harbour, but that's not what ships are for."

WILLIAM G.T. SHEDD

Rating questions are popular with coaches because they quickly give us a gauge of progress.

But on a scale of 1-10, 7 is a problem.

It's safe, it's average.

It's saying that we're not doing badly, but we're not excelling either.

7 is a great number to choose if you don't want to be overly self-critical.

7 is a way to escape a potentially difficult but important conversation.

In order to know what work we need to do, we need a truly honest score.

As an Authoritative Coach, when you are asking rating questions, eliminate 7 as an option and challenge people to pick a 6 or an 8.

If it's a 6, what are we ignoring? Where are we lacking? Where do we need to step up?

If it's an 8, what have we done to truly deserve an 8?

I use scorecards as the foundation of my coaching programs, and here's an example of how I phrase the question:

"On a scale of 1-10, with 1 being 'we're failing' and 10 being 'we're world class and this has truly become part of our culture', how would you rate your ability to consistently produce high quality They Ask, You Answer content? And you can't choose 7."

Or, if you are doing the scoring activity asynchronously, you can add:

"...you can't choose 7. If you feel tempted to answer with a 7, ask yourself, is it really a 6 and we've clearly got work to do to show that we're truly performing in this category, or is it an 8 and I can prove why we deserve an 8 in this category? And so, I don't want to see any 7s in your results. We want an honest and realistic score that helps us get clear on the work we need to do our best work."

Try this out next time you are asking a 1–10 rating question and see what difference it makes to the quality of your coaching conversations.

Don't forget, it's not necessarily the score that matters here, but the coaching conversation it allows you to facilitate.

33

ENDING MEETINGS

"We do not learn from experience...we learn from reflecting on experience."

JOHN DEWEY

I was asked this question recently: How do you know that the people in your coaching sessions are getting value from the work you are doing together?

The answer is simple: I ask them.

It doesn't happen in every single session, but I do try to make time as much as possible to wrap up my sessions in the same way, allowing every person the opportunity to articulate and share what's been the most useful for them.

You can phrase it in different ways:

- What's the one thing you are taking away from this session

today?
- What's been the single most useful lesson for you today?
- What's one thing you are going to implement immediately following this session today?
- What's been the single greatest insight from our time together today?

You might be thinking, "what if they have nothing to share?" Based on my experience across 1000s of hours of coaching, you really have nothing to worry about; I have never had anyone refuse to answer or have nothing to share at the end of my sessions.

Even when I feel like I didn't have a great session, there's always something valuable.

I enjoy listening to everyone share what they received from our time together, but that's not why I do it.

Before they leave the session, I want everyone to have the opportunity to reflect on what we've just covered and then articulate it, with the intention that they are more likely to remember it and take action.

Are you making time to wrap up your coaching or leadership sessions in a way that allows everyone to contribute?

34

ENDING RELATIONSHIPS

"A good ending is vital to a picture, the single most important element, because it is what the audience takes with them out of the theatre."

WALT DISNEY

There's nothing that frustrates me more than watching people botch endings. We're mostly terrible at this across the whole of our lives, and our work with our coaching clients is no exception.

I recently had a great final coaching call with a client, and these are the questions that I used to make the ending a truly great experience for all of us:

- In what ways is the company different now than it was XX months ago?
- What are you the most proud of?
- What has been your greatest achievement over the past XX

months?
- What's something you learned about yourself?
- What could cause you to fail here and undo all this great work you've done over the past XX months?
- What needs to continue to be true X months from now that will make sure this work sticks?
- Going forward, what do you believe to be your top 3 priorities?

Take the time to think about what a great ending should look like.

Ideally, endings should be well planned so they add to the client experience and we all finish on a high.

IV

MASTERY

As Marcus mentioned, "To err is human, and unless each of us goes back to the well and keeps drinking, bad habits can form quickly in our behaviour." Just like high performing athletes who attend their practice sessions every day, you must treat your work in the same way if you want to be truly indispensable to your clients. You will become a 'detached observer' of your work so you can objectively see where you can improve. You love the work and enjoy practice for the sake of practice itself.

35

TURN UP

"I have learned one thing. As Woody says, 'Showing up is 80 percent of life.' Sometimes it's easier to hide at home in bed. I've done both."

MARSHALL BRICKMAN

My dad is a competitive runner, and he recently won an important race that put him in top place for his age category in Scotland.

But he didn't feel like going — he had to drive a fair distance, the weather was bad, he had a few small injuries, and he wasn't running at his best.

He also knew that at least two of his main competitors would be there, and realistically they would beat him in the race.

Plenty of reasons to not bother going.

How often do you have fleeting thoughts that attempt to rationalise why you shouldn't turn up for work?

I have them more than I'd like — I'm tired, I don't feel 100%, I don't want to do it, no one is waiting for it, it can wait until tomorrow, it's not important, etc...

In The War of Art[23], Steven Pressfield calls this **Resistance** — a negative force in the world that keeps you from fulfilling your dreams.

I hate having these kinds of thoughts, but I've learned how to deal with them quickly so they don't get the better of me.

And I often think about how my dad ended up winning this race.

So, what happened?

Well, even though he knew he wouldn't win, and he wouldn't run at his best, the most important step was getting in his car, driving through the bad weather, and arriving at the venue in time for the race.

In other words, he showed up.

What he couldn't have predicted, though, was that fortune was waiting for him at the venue.

When he stepped up to his starting blocks he noticed that the two competitors he was worried about hadn't turned up! Placing him in the strongest position to win the race.

Why didn't they turn up? Did Resistance get the better of them that day? I wonder if they had the same thoughts as my dad?

My dad went on to win the race and take the top place in his age category.

Even though he didn't want to go, he turned up anyway.

When I have these fleeting thoughts that are attempting to stop me from turning up, I know exactly what I need to do.

I need to show up.

I need to make a start.

What I've learned is that I can't rely on feeling motivated in order to show up for work. **Motivation shows up when I show up.**

Just like my dad. He turned up and fortune met him when he got there, which unquestionably motivated him to race better.

So what's the rub?

Don't let your negative thoughts sabotage you.

Don't let them stop your best work.

When they come, see them as a calling.

Then turn up.

And do the work.

Personal Reflection

- How important is it for me to turn up, even if I don't feel like it?
- What thoughts or excuses get in the way of me turning up and doing my best work?
- What am I waiting for?

36

REPS

"Between the idea
And the reality
Between the motion
And the act
Falls the Shadow"
T.S. ELIOT

Most good companies provide excellent training opportunities, but what they're not so great at is creating a suitable environment for practice — to allow people to 'get their reps in'.

Let me try and help out here with a non-work related experience...

I popped over to the U.S. for a few weeks, and over the weekend I got to spend some quality time with Marcus Sheridan and his family.

One of the family rituals is that every weekend they play 18-holes of disc golf. And this time around, I was fortunate enough to be able to take part.

I've never played before. In fact, I'm not really a sporty person.

As we're getting prepared to play the game, I started worrying about all the things you'd imagine — mostly that I'd suck and hold everyone else back, and because of that no one would enjoy the experience.

But, they did something that created a learning environment that meant I could suck and still enjoy myself.

We created two teams of three:

- One person was great
- One person was good
- One person was a beginner (me!)

All three of us on the team got to play the full game, and we got a shot at each hole until we finished, but...after every shot was taken, **we led from the best of the three throws from the team.**

It was perfect for me. I could suck, and it didn't matter. I could have fun and not worry about holding everyone else back.

I started to let go...

Interestingly, it wasn't until about halfway through the course that I actually stopped trying to be good. After nine holes of trying to look like I knew what I was doing, I started to let go.

I had one magical moment towards the end where I had completely given up trying and the disc glided into the net, and I won a hole for our team.

I didn't think it was such a big deal until everyone jumped on me and we celebrated the shot together.

It was really cool.

So, what am I getting at?

I was able to suck while getting my reps in. I was able to take what I was being taught and make dozens of mistakes. And, I was able to do it without any consequence to the game or my team.

I had permission to suck.

And what's interesting to me is that even with the permission, it still took me a while to let myself make mistakes and potentially fail.

I was given the space to practice.

I'd like you to consider how you are setting up your own working environment:

- Am I giving myself the room to practice?
- Am I giving myself the permission to fail and make mistakes?
- Am I able to get my reps in?
- Do I have the room and the permission to suck without feeling like I'm letting my clients down?

Just like a tennis coach that tosses you 100 backhands to practice before you play the big game, how are we giving yourself the room to practice?

I've learned this from coaching dozens of leaders and businesses: The biggest opportunity we all have is practising our communication skills so we can be more confident and competent in high-stakes situations.

Personal Reflection

Having read this far you will now start to see client situations in a different light. Things that you were once unaware of, will become obvious, unacceptable, and clear areas for improvement.

Your job as the best communicator in the room, is to be able to spot where you and your team can improve. Here are a few key prompts to help you look for areas to practice becoming an Authoritative Coach - identify specific scenarios to work on:

1. How often do I have net-negative meetings with clients and prospects? What's causing friction? What's slowing

down momentum?

2. How often do I find myself stuck and thrown off by a difficult question or objection from a client, and then find it difficult to recover in the moment?
3. How often do I shy away from giving direct feedback to my clients, instead sweeping it under the carpet — only to see that problem arise later?
4. How often do I get defensive or stuck, and find it difficult to solve a client problem?
5. How often do I simply say 'yes' to an idea, request, or scope issue that I should have said 'no' to?
6. How often do I let my clients make mistakes that I know will hurt them later?

Create the space and seek out the high-stakes conversations and scenarios to practice, so when it comes to the real situation, you can be the best communicator in the room.

37

TENSIONS

"It's not what the vision is, it's what the vision does."

ROBERT FRITZ

When it comes to learning and development, you and I see the world differently than most, and I want you to know that just because other people don't completely understand you, you are not the problem.

This 'journey' that you are on is exactly where you need to be.

There's something uniquely different about you compared to other people, and it's time to understand what it is so you can fully embrace it.

A while back you made a commitment to a life of learning

It became a mindset, then a discipline, and then your identity.

You created a vision for a better future for you and the people around you. You said "I want to be the best I can be," and you created a gap, a tension between your current reality and your vision.

This tension drives you every day to work on becoming a better person and doing your best work. This 'force' is an absolute requirement for the pursuit of personal mastery. You will never quite reach your vision — this tension will always be there.

You must get comfortable with it and use it to propel you to your vision — it's your ally, not your enemy.

However, as with anything under tension, there is more than one way to release it — you can either rise to your vision or lower your vision to your current reality.

It's the insidious nature of your emotions that will be the reason why you might lower your goal and pull your vision down to your current reality.

This 'emotional tension' includes all the reasons why you can't succeed — the belief that you don't deserve it, that you aren't capable.

To succeed, you must cultivate a high tolerance for this 'emotional tension'.

You must distinguish between the creative force you have

created and the self-doubt. They are not the same thing. They conflict with each other — one pulling you to your vision, the other pulling you away.

What will help you to succeed is sustaining a high level of comfort for long-term delayed gratification.

The thing is, you're never going to be 'done'

You will never 'arrive.' And so, to succeed and get closer to making your vision your reality, you must get comfortable living and working in this world of creative and emotional tensions pulling upon you.

You have to be comfortable never quite getting there — staying in your current reality while at the same time knowing that your best work and your best years are ahead of you.

The other option doesn't bear thinking about.

Know this: Only mediocre people are always at their best.

Personal Reflection:

- What is it that motivates me to want to be better and improve my professional skills? Why do this work?
- What would happen if I didn't invest in my professional development?
- Do I accept that, through the creation of my own ambition, I am personally responsible for bringing tensions into my life?

38

PROGRESS

"It's time you realised that you have something in you more powerful and miraculous than the things that affect you and make you dance like a puppet"

MARCUS AURELIUS

I've been learning from and studying the Stoics for over 10 years. Their timeless wisdom from ~2000 years ago has helped me across all areas of my life and continues to be the foundation of my philosophy for life and business.

The Stoics took learning and development seriously — making sure, as far as possible, that their words matched their actions, that they lived a life of virtue and integrity, and that they helped others through teaching — mostly through lectures.

One thing they knew for sure is that there's no end to learning.

Becoming a 'wise sage' was an ideal, rather than a realistic goal to achieve.

We are all a work in progress.

I'd love to share *all* my favourite passages with you, and perhaps I can do that over time, but for now, I've picked out three quotes that have helped me to think differently about how we learn and what we do with what we're learning - how we study, practice, and eventually make it our own.

"To read attentively — not to be satisfied with just getting the gist of it" — Marcus Aurelius, Meditations 1.7

We can translate this into anything that we're learning: A book, an online class, an in-person lecture.

We should think more critically about what we're learning. We don't simply take it all at face value — we peel back the layers, dig deep and get to the root.

Learning is not passive. To be a student means to actively study the material.

As a result, we become much more active in what we're learning, and what we're learning has real structure, depth, and understanding.

Yes, it's slower, it takes more time, but it proves to be much more valuable and fulfiling.

We live in a surface-level world telling us to learn more, to learn faster, to tell everyone what we're learning and how much progress we're making. If we can learn to ignore all of that, we might just be able to enjoy learning for its own sake.

"Those who receive the bare theories immediately want to spew them, as an upset stomach does its food. First digest your theories and you won't throw them up." — Epictetus, Discourses, 3.21.1-3

How often do we see people spouting out regurgitated facts and theories on LinkedIn? Or talking about this new course they are doing or the book they are reading? You can tell that it's too early — they haven't taken any time to truly understand how it impacts their work.

They sound smart, but are they *good*?

What this means for us is to take what we are studying and sit with it. Resist the temptation to share it with others just to look smart or better. Hold back on telling the world what we're doing right now.

Internalise it all, and let it show up through your work. Let it make you a better CEO, coach, leader, or manager.

Even better: Let others talk about how much better you've become.

"We should hunt out the helpful pieces of teaching and the spirited and noble-minded sayings which are capable of immediate practical application...and learn them so well that words become works." — Seneca, Letters from a Stoic, CVIII

What have we got so far? We make smart choices about what we're learning and studying, we think more critically, we then internalise what we're learning, and then...?

What Seneca is saying here is, yes, go to the sources, read the books, learn from people that have come before you — but do the work and turn it into something of your own doing.

We take what we've learned, we put it to work, and we get *our* stories, *our* results, *our* version of that thing.

Now it belongs to you.

Once we get here, it's time to share with the world what you've learned, because you've now turned it into a unique work of your own.

Final thoughts

Becoming a Stoic practitioner has taught me to slow down, do the work, and not get distracted by the noise of the world and other people's progress. To find happiness and satisfaction in the learning, and to let it affect my work in a way that puts me in a better position to help more people in better ways.

It's a daily discipline to resist instant gratification and the temptations of people's approval — to not just continually spout out whatever thought you have on your mind today. I like to think I'm doing my part by only sharing and teaching what has come from something of my own doing.

As coaches we resist the need for instant gratification, for public recognition and praise.

When I first read these passages I knew I was on to something important. I feel even more invigorated now after writing and sharing it with you.

You're doing the right thing by taking your learning and professional development seriously — making good choices, taking your time, and enjoying the process of learning to become a better coach.

One of the common traits of the best coaches in the world, is that they are on a journey to personal mastery, and they've made their professional development a priority.

Marcus, Seneca, and Epictetus would be proud.

Personal Reflection

- Do I treat personal mastery as a priority? If not, how does that play out in the long term?
- Does my weekly schedule support my need to learn and grow? Where do I need to protect my time?
- How is my need for permission holding me back from

producing something I can call my own?

39

ENVIRONMENT

“Part of my joy in learning is that it puts me in a position to teach; nothing however outstanding and however helpful, will ever give me any pleasure if the knowledge is to be for my benefit alone.”

SENECA

A while back I was playing at the local park with my stepson, Paddy, when he tried out the monkey bars for the first time.

He tried a few times but he couldn’t get past the first rung. He kept falling off before even attempting to reach for the second rung. It was clear to me that he couldn’t quite figure out the technique required to move forward.

A few moments later, a slightly older girl appeared on the scene. She was much more confident and managed the monkey bars without any hesitation.

As Paddy watched the older girl effortlessly make her way across the five rungs, he knew at that moment that he could do it.

It was one of those special moments of self-awareness as I watched Paddy shifting from feeling **frustrated**, **defeated**, and **upset** about failing, to feeling **confident**, **believing in himself** and **celebrating his success** when he made it to the end.

This all took place in just a few minutes.

The dynamics of learning

Let's take a closer look at the learning dynamic between Paddy, the girl, and the monkey bars.

Paddy, who had several failed attempts, observed the older girl on the monkey bars and learned two things.

- First, that it was possible to go all the way to the end of the five rungs.
- Second, the technique required to do it. He now had a teacher, or mentor, to show him how.

The difference between what a learner can do without help and what he or she can do with help is called the "Zone of Proximal Development[24]" or ZPD.

The ZPD for Paddy was to go from not being able to do the monkey bars, to getting to the end successfully. In this case the zone was identified, and then a 'mentor' arrived to help coach and assist him through the gap to the point where he could do it.

This technique for learning is also referred to as "scaffolding." This is where the teacher supports and helps you while you learn something until you reach the point where you can do it successfully with minimal assistance.

Then, they remove the scaffolding so you can perform the activity on your own.

What can we learn from Paddy's story?

First, the slightly older girl was not an expert. She only knew a little more than Paddy did. For all we know, a few weeks ago the girl might not have been able to do the monkey bars at all. Perhaps more importantly, it wouldn't be the same learning experience if Paddy had observed me doing the monkey bars. Regardless of whether I can do it or not, I'm a lot older and stronger and Paddy can't relate to me as an adult.

Second, Paddy was heavily involved in his own learning. He wasn't told how to do the monkey bars. He observed, tried, failed, and tried again.

In Range[25], David Epstein writes "*Frustration is not a sign you aren't learning, but ease is.*"

Epstein also shows that repetition is less important than the struggle, and that learning slowly is part of the journey: "*It is difficult to accept that the best learning road is slow, and that doing poorly now is essential for better performance later.*"

Similarly, Paddy struggled through the process, which in turn strengthened the learning process for him.

Today, we are far too concerned about getting the answer quickly and getting a head start that we sacrifice our own learning as a result.

Most people I know would find this narrative challenging. They want their knowledge fast — and want learning to happen instantly before their eyes.

Third, Paddy built self-belief and confidence by seeing someone else achieve it first, and from observing someone very close to his stage in development.

Finally, it's worth noting that Paddy would probably have learned the monkey bars himself eventually, without help. But it would have taken him a lot longer.

We shouldn't only consider what we are capable of on our own; just like Paddy, we learn best when we are in a social setting: a learning environment.

Humans are social creatures, and our learning is enhanced when we share the process with others.

Personal Reflection

- Are my expectations for my learning aligned correctly? Am I prepared to work through the struggle, or am I expecting my learning to come quick and easy?
- Have I surrounded myself with the right mentors people that will challenge me to grow and improve?
- Where do I have the opportunity to be the mentor to others where I'm only one or two steps ahead?
- What do I need to do to create the ideal learning environment so I can do my best work?

Join The Authoritative Coaching Community: www.theauthoritativecoach.co.uk[26]

V

THE CHOICE

As an Authoritative Coach you will continually strive for better. Every new client is an opportunity to start anew. To upgrade your clients. To do better work. To be a better coach. To have even greater success than what's come before. And so, get your head in the game, take your position, do the work, and learn from the challenges you come up against. The work is never done, but it must also start somewhere, and that's up to you - to choose what kind of coach you want to be.

40

IT'S NOT ABOUT YOU

"Your vision will become clear only when you can look into your own heart. Who looks outside, dreams; who looks inside, awakes."

CARL JUNG

At the request of my mentor, I made my way up to the front of the stage to deliver my feedback to a practising public speaker.

From that point onward it's all a blur.

I thought I was ready for this. But I was completely out of my depth.

I was stumbling, fumbling and failing.

I felt like a fraud.

My job as the understudy was to observe my mentor at work, think about how I would coach in the same situation, and then compare notes.

Up until this point I thought I was making significant progress with my communication and coaching skills.

This was shaping up to be the most difficult and humbling experience in my career so far, but it ultimately led me to the breakthrough I had been searching for.

On the second day, after a difficult morning, I had to take a time out.

A breather.

I shuffled into the middle of the theatre and found a seat deep in the shadows and observed my mentor work from a distance.

"What is it that he can see that I can't see?"

"Will I ever be able to do this?"

"Is it even possible to learn whatever this is?"

Even though I was on the brink of giving up hope, I started to think about what was taking place right in front of me:

- My mentor was completely focused on the person he's coaching
- He was able to say exactly what he saw

- He was not worried about being wrong

Where does this all come from? How can he be so confident and self-assured?

My ego was getting in my way

I began to understand — and I started to see where my time on stage had been a failure.

- I was trying too hard to be right.
- I was too invested in how I looked in front of the audience.
- I was making it all about me.

It's not a lack of skills or knowledge. It was my ego that was getting in my way.

Curious about this self-discovery, I asked my mentor where he learned to become such a great communicator. He never learned this in a classroom with workbooks and step-by-step guides — it had been through decades of experiences and self-development.

It turns out that I've been looking in all the wrong places.

What I needed to do was look in the mirror. To stop looking for the answers externally, and look within:

- Who am I?
- What do I believe?
- What are my values?

- Who do I want to be?
- What's important to me?

And so for over five years, that's what I've been working on, and I'm working even harder on it today than ever before. This work never ends.

I'm forever grateful to my great friend and mentor Marcus Sheridan for seeing the potential in me, coaching me, and providing me the opportunity to work with people all over the world.

In my work today, I see coaches, leaders and managers struggling with the same challenges that I was trying to figure out five years ago — trying too hard, needing to be right, getting in their own way — and they are held back from their true potential because of their approach.

Stop trying to control everything. Let it happen. Focus on the other person, and...

...don't make it about you.

AUTHORITATIVE COACH MANIFESTO

"I now realise that my need to be liked is holding me and my clients back from succeeding at our highest potential."

THE AUTHORITATIVE COACH

Choose coaching. Choose guiding people to reach their highest potential. Choose staring down the hard truths of character and ambition, and deciding whether a client's got the grit or they're just taking up space.

Choose sizing them up, making the call whether they're a good fit for your style, a fit for your vision. Choose being bold enough to say, "You're not ready," if they're not.

Choose no longer sitting on the sidelines, watching as they blunder into every mistake in the book. Choose the brutal honesty, the brutal kindness of 'Radical Candor.'

Choose being led by your curiosity, speaking your mind, saying the things they can't or won't hear from anyone else. Choose digging deep, peeling back the layers of deception and deflection until the raw truth of the problem is laid bare.

Choose respect over likeability. You don't need them to be

your friend, you need them to do the work. Choose leaving the smartest-person-in-the-room complex at the door.

Choose making your clients the heroes of their own narratives, the masters of their own destinies. Choose firing off pointed questions, short and sharp, demanding answers that resonate.

Choose being the master of communication, knowing when to step back, when to nudge forward. Choose holding your own against the pressure, stepping confidently into the awkward silences and tension-filled exchanges.

Choose redirecting the problems, accountability, and responsibility back to them, letting them grapple, grow, and gain insight.

Choose questioning assumptions, choosing verification over blind trust. Choose to not take it personally, because it's not about you. It's about them.

Choose accepting that the work is never over. You're in for the long haul. Choose your path. Choose coaching. **Choose to be an Authoritative Coach.**

* * *

Get a printed version of the manifesto

Email chris@theauthoritativecoach.co.uk and request a printable copy of the Authoritative Coach Manifesto. Once you've pinned it up in your coaching space, take a picture and tag me on Instagram @theauthoritativecoach[27].

CAN YOU HELP?

"Be so busy giving others recognition that you don't really need it for yourself."

JIM ROHN

One of the milestones I'm looking forward to celebrating as a first-time author is the moment when someone I've never met or worked with picks up the book and finds it valuable.

Amazon reviews are perhaps the most important factor that influence someone's decision to buy a non-fiction book. Your review of *Become an Authoritative Coach* will help people that have never heard of me or the book get a sense of why it'll be worth it.

Will you take the time to post a review on Amazon?

To help you along, here are a few prompts to build your review around:

- In your own words, what does it mean to you to be an Authoritative Coach?
- In what way will the book help you to be more valuable to your clients?

- What has been your single most valuable lesson from the book?
- Why should someone who's discovering this book for the first time buy it and read it?

Let's help more coaches and leaders step into their authority so they can be in the very best position to help their clients do their best work and be successful at their highest potential.

Thank you,

Chris.

THIS WORK NEVER ENDS

"Stop thinking 'I should have started years ago.' That's failure thinking. Instead think, 'I'm going to start now, my best years are ahead of me.' That's the way successful people think.

DAVID J. SCHWARTZ

Even as I was preparing the final manuscript for this book, I was writing new material that could have easily become a new chapter or section, and it reminded me that this work will never feel like it's done.

It's a continual work in progress for all of us.

With that in mind, I'd like to encourage you to follow my latest writing and continue this important work together at www.theauthoritativecoach.co.uk[28]

* * *

For speaking, podcast and coaching enquiries:

- chris@theauthoritativecoach.co.uk[29]
- LinkedIn: @theauthoritativecoach[30]

GRATITUDE

"You can call me anything that you want, but don't ever, ever call me a self-made man."

ARNOLD SCHWARZENEGGER

On 26th September 2019 I closed down my business and I literally had no idea what I was going to do next. It was one of those defining moments in life where I had to first let go of the smaller cup I was holding on to so I could grab the next larger one.

Late that same evening at 1 am, I sent a message to my mentor and friend, Marcus Sheridan, to let him know about my decision. He said "I'm glad to hear that, because I've felt like it has been holding you back for a long time."

This was the day that Marcus invited me to join him at his agency - IMPACT. He raised the stakes and gave me the opportunity to do a higher level of coaching, with larger companies, all over the world, at a far greater volume. I was able to get my reps in, make my mistakes, and ultimately unlock my true coaching ability.

Without Marcus and his They Ask, You Answer methodology

you would not be reading these words today.

Thank you, Marcus, for your mentorship, your patience and believing in me. You are the wind in my sails.

SELECTED READING LIST

"For books continue each other, in spite of our habit of judging them separately."

VIRGINIA WOOLF

This isn't so much of a bibliography, but rather a nod to the authors and their books that helped shape how I think about the kind of coach I want to be.

For avid readers, this section is often one of the most valuable parts of a book.

Over the course of many years, the words in the following books dripped into my coaching practice, and through 1000s of hours of coaching I was able to make those words my own, which then ultimately became the book you are reading today.

Become an Authoritative Coach is my interpretation of everything I've learned from others, and I hope that it's a worthy contribution to the world of non-fiction writing and represents everyone that has come before me in the best way.

Find out what I'm reading now on Goodreads[31]

* * *

They Ask, You Answer, *by Marcus Sheridan*

Mastery, *by Robert Greene*

The Laws of Human Nature, *by Robert Greene*

The 48 Laws of Power, *by Robert Greene*

The Obstacle is the Way, *by Ryan Holiday*

Ego is the Enemy, *by Ryan Holiday*

The Daily Stoic, *by Ryan Holiday*

Meditations, *by Marcus Aurelius*

Letters from a Stoic, *by Seneca*

The Fifth Discipline, *by Peter Senge*

The Inner Game of Tennis, *by W. Timothy Gallwey*

Range, *by David Epstein*

Deep Work, *by Cal Newport*

Radical Candor, *by Kim Scott*

The HeART of Laser Focused Coaching, *by Marion Franklin*

The Four Agreements, *by Don Miguel Ruiz*

The War of Art, *by Steven Pressfield*

Exactly What to Say, *by Phil M. Jones*

The Coaching Habit, *by Michael Bungay Stanier*

Dare to Lead, *by Brene Brown*

Tuesdays with Morrie, *by Mitch Albom*

Coach, *by Michael Lewis*

Indistractable, *by Nir Eyal*

The Artist's Way, *by Julia Cameron*

Pitch Anything, *by Oren Klaff*

PRAISE FOR CHRIS MARR

"If you want to grow your business as a CEO, business leader, or entrepreneur, I recommend working with Chris Marr. During the last three years, Chris has been instrumental in AES making the Inc 5000 list each year and helping us achieve a three-year CAGR of 115%. What I love about Chris's approach is his style of Socratic coaching. He asks the better questions to help me discover and challenge everyone at AES to be the best version of themselves. Chris helped me improve my communication, including asking questions when working with customers. He has enabled everyone at AES to become a better communicator, a key to connecting and knowing our customers better than anyone else in our market. I am incredibly grateful for his coaching style and his help in helping me improve as a leader." - **Jim Scultz**, *Founder and CEO, Applied Educational Systems (AES)*

"Chris has been a coach and mentor to me for a few years now. His experience and guidance has been profound both personally and professionally. If there's one thing Chris wants for you, it's to succeed in life and business. He brings a wealth of wisdom and knowledge to the table like no other. He listens and cares deeply. He'll challenge and support you to your greatest. If you want to achieve incredible things that you didn't even think were possible - Chris is exactly who you should be working with." - **Nicola Crawford**, *Sales and Marketing Director, Gillies* *and Mackay*

"Our team engaged with Chris to conduct training and coaching on delivering world class communication and using video and assignment selling to improve our sales techniques. Throughout this training I learned how to better structure my communication with prospects and clients, how to reduce weak language to be a more effective communicator, and how to embrace every communication as an opportunity to further educate my audience. Aside from helping me become a better communicator, his coaching has helped me become more comfortable in asking for and receiving feedback from my peers on my videos and emails, and has helped shorten my sales cycle. Chris' teaching style is collaborative while also engaging everyone individually to consider what's working, where they struggle, and how he can help them to succeed. He leads with thought-provoking questions which spur important discussions, enabling our team to quickly identify key areas to work on. We are incredibly grateful for his guidance, coaching and support." - **Kaitlyn Pintarich**, *Owner and President, Berry Insurance*

Connect with Chris on LinkedIn: @theauthoritativecoach[32]

Notes

ABOUT THE AUTHOR

1 Exclusive subscription offer for readers: https://www.theauthoritativecoach.co.uk/subscribe?coupon=65d28d3c

2 For speaking, podcast and coaching enquiries, email chris@theauthoritativecoach.co.uk

3 Chris Marr on LinkedIn: https://www.linkedin.com/in/theauthoritativecoach

DEFINITION

4 Google search result: "Define authoritative"

FOREWORD

5 Marcus Sheridan, Author of They Ask, You Answer: https://www.goodreads.com/book/show/30557185-they-ask-you-answer

THE PRIZE

6 Mad Men Clip: https://youtu.be/OwwFd6iA6rI (YouTube search term: *Don Draper dealing with a client objection*)

7 Pitch Anything, by Oren Klaff: https://www.goodreads.com/book/show/10321016-pitch-anything

BEING 'RADICALLY CANDID' - PART I

8 The Radical Candor Framework is a trademark of Radical Candor, LLC.

Radical Candor was created by Kim Scott. You have been introduced to the framework as part of developing your authoritative positioning. If you want to learn more, please see the following resources from Kim Scott and her organisation.

Free Radical Candor resources: https://www.radicalcandor.com/resources

Radical Candor in 6 minutes, with Kim Scott: https://youtu.be/YLBDkz0TwLM

The Feedback Loop (Online Course): https://www.radicalcandor.com/resources

Radical Candor, by Kim Scott (Book): https://www.goodreads.com/book/show/29939161-radical-candor

BEING 'RADICALLY CANDID' - PART II

9 The Radical Candor Framework is a trademark of Radical Candor, LLC.

The Radical Candor framework: https://www.radicalcandor.com/our-approach/

WHY NOW?

10 The Choice, by Edith Eger: https://www.goodreads.com/book/show/30753738-the-choice

PROBLEMS

11 An introduction to The Drama Triangle: https://youtu.be/E_XSeUYa0-8

RESPONSIBILITY

12 Contributed by Zach Basner: https://www.linkedin.com/in/zachary-basner/

PERSON VS STORY - PART II

13 The Inner Game of Tennis, by W. Timothy Gallwey: https://www.goodreads.com/book/show/905.The_Inner_Game_of_Tennis

DISARM

14 7 Habits of Highly Effective People, by Stephen Covey: https://www.goodreads.com/book/show/55533315-the-7-habits-of-highly-effective-people

WHAT VS WHY

15 The HeART of Laser Focused Coaching, by Marion Franklin: https://www.goodreads.com/book/show/52153407-the-heart-of-laser-focused-coaching

ASK WHY TO VERIFY

16 Contributed by Brian Casey: https://www.linkedin.com/in/brian-p-casey/

MISTAKES

17 The Death of Expertise, by Thomas M. Nichols: https://www.goodreads.com/book/show/34055054-the-death-of-expertise

FOCUS

18 7 Habits of Highly Effective People, by Stephen Covey: https://www.goodreads.com/book/show/55533315-the-7-habits-of-highly-effective-people

WE'RE NOT DONE YET

19 What is They Ask, You Answer?: https://www.impactplus.com/what-is-they-ask-you-answer

20 A brief guide to SMART goals: https://www.atlassian.com/blog/productivity/how-to-write-smart-goals

21 IMPACT: https://www.impactplus.com

22 Digital Sales and Marketing Scorecard: https://www.impactplus.com/scorecard

TURN UP

23 The War of Art, by Steven Pressfield: https://www.goodreads.com/book/show/1319.The_War_of_Art

ENVIRONMENT

24 The Zone of Proximal Development: https://en.wikipedia.org/wiki/Zone_of_proximal_development

25 Range, by David Epstein: https://www.goodreads.com/book/show/41795733-range

26 The Authoritative Coaching Community: www.theauthoritativecoach.co.uk

AUTHORITATIVE COACH MANIFESTO

27 The Authoritative Coach on Instagram: https://www.instagram.com/theauthoritativecoach/

THIS WORK NEVER ENDS

28 Exclusive subscription offer for readers: https://www.theauthoritativecoach.co.uk/subscribe?coupon=65d28d3c

29 For speaking, podcast and coaching enquiries, email chris@theauthoritativecoach.co.uk

30 Chris Marr on LinkedIn: https://www.linkedin.com/in/theauthoritativecoach

SELECTED READING LIST

31 Follow Chris Marr on Goodreads: https://www.goodreads.com/author/show/42105499.Chris_Marr

PRAISE FOR CHRIS MARR

32 Chris Marr on LinkedIn: https://www.linkedin.com/in/theauthoritativecoach

Printed in Great Britain
by Amazon

26695659R10099